"Who is like the Lord?"

The Meaning of Micah

By Charles Ozanne

ISBN: 978-1-78364-511-4

www.obt.org.uk

****

THE OPEN BIBLE TRUST
Fordland Mount, Upper Basildon,
Reading, RG8 8LU, UK.

"Who is like the Lord?"

The Meaning of Micah

Contents

Introduction

Introduction

The nation of Israel reached its zenith under the kingship of David and Solomon. But in the latter part of Solomon's reign he was influenced by his foreign wives and allowed idolatry to exist side by side with the worship of the LORD. And he "did what was evil in the sight of the LORD and did not wholly follow the LORD, as David his father had" (1 Kings 11:1-6). As a result of this, the LORD split his kingdom, leaving his son, Rehoboam, as king over only one tribe (Judah, later to be joined by Benjamin).

From this point onwards the nation of Israel was divided between ten Northern tribes and two Southern tribes (1 Kings 11:30-40). They were identified as "the house of Israel and the house of Judah" (Jeremiah 31:31). Hence there were two lines of kings, reigning side by side over the two 'houses'. During this period the LORD raised up various prophets to speak to these two kingdoms. This was the situation when the LORD called Micah to prophesy to His people.

The prophet Micah, from Moresheth, prophesied in the reigns of Jotham, Ahaz, and Hezekiah, kings of Judah. He was prophesying therefore between about 740 and 700 BC, possibly even longer. Isaiah, his great contemporary, prophesied in the reigns of the same three kings, but he began a little earlier than Micah, in the reign of Uzziah (Azariah) (Isaiah 1:1). These two prophets confirm and complement one another. They major on the same themes and they are both preoccupied with the person of Christ. Hosea prophesied in the Northern Kingdom in the reigns of the same four kings; likewise Amos and Joel in the earlier period when Jeroboam II was reigning in Israel and Uzziah in Judah. Hence there was no shortage of preachers at that time, exposing the wickedness of the people and the terrible consequences of their rebellion. But their explicit warnings of coming retribution fell by and large on deaf ears.

Amos from Tekoa and Nahum the Elkoshite are also identified by their places of origin. Others (Isaiah, Jeremiah, Ezekiel, Hosea, Joel, Jonah, Zephaniah, and Zechariah) are identified by naming their fathers. These were known and respected members of the community, unlike the lowly prophets whom the Lord plucked from Moresheth and Tekoa. Micah is identified by the place he came from. That was Moresheth, the same probably as Moresheth-gath in 1:14, a village some 25 miles south-west of Jerusalem. "Such an identification would be given to a man away from home by others who marked him with the name of the place from which he came", says James Mays[1]. Micah hailed from Moresheth but was prophesying for the most part in Jerusalem, it seems, but he also had a message for the Northern Kingdom.

The name Micah is short for Micaiah (*Mi-ka-yah*) as he is called in Jeremiah 26:18 (Hebrew). It means "Who is like the Lord?" He alludes to his own name in 7:18, "Who is God like you?"(*Mi El kamoka.*) Part of the answer is given in the same verse, "pardoning iniquity and passing over transgression", and some more in Exodus 15:11, "Who is like you, O Lord, among the gods? Who is like you, majestic in holiness, awesome in glorious deeds, doing wonders?" It is "an exclamation of praise, an expression of adoration and wonder at the incomparable God of Israel" (Mays)[2].

Micah's prophecies provide abundant evidence of the truth expressed in Micah's name. His detailed predictions of future

---

[1] James L Mays, *Micah, A Commentary*, 1976, p15.
[2] Mays, p1.

events, including the birth of the Lord Jesus at Bethlehem, are proof enough of his peerless nature and incomparable wisdom.

The prophets however were not exclusively predictors of the future. Their primary function was that of preachers, men who exposed the cancer of sin and proclaimed the terrible punishment which could only be avoided by repentance and radical reform. They were the nation's conscience as well as proclaimers of God's word in judgment and mercy. This aspect of their ministry may seem wearisome to us especially when it is protracted, but we need to remember that most of what they say (in principle at least) is applicable to our own society. Our nation is deserving of judgement even if, by God's grace, it is deferred for the time being. Western society is deeply stricken with the same cancer of stubborn unbelief as we are all too aware.

Micah states his commission in 3:8, "I am filled with power, with the Spirit of the Lord, and with justice and might, to declare to Jacob his transgression and to Israel his sin." That however is only half the story. He was also sent to declare to Israel their prophetic destiny: the destruction of both Samaria (the capital of the Northern Kingdom, Israel) and Jerusalem (the capital of the Southern Kingdom of Judah) and the latter's exile to Babylon, the birth and rule of their Messiah, their return from exile, the annihilation of the godless "Assyrian", and the glorious days to follow. A huge vista opens before our eyes, beginning in the eighth century BC and stretching way into the future. Only in Isaiah do we find the same breadth and length of vision and revelation.

Micah is especially significant as exemplifying principles of prophetic interpretation. Two in particular come to mind: the principle of postponed fulfilment and the principle of cumulative fulfilment. The destruction of Jerusalem was predicted in and for the reign of Hezekiah, but because Hezekiah repented and entreated the favour of the Lord the judgment was postponed for a later time. This is spelt out for us in Jeremiah 26:16-19. When eventually the prophecy was fulfilled more than 130 years later (in 586 BC) there were elements which remained unfulfilled. The last ounce was not squeezed from this prophecy until AD 135 after the Bar-Cochba rebellion. The same principle of cumulative fulfilment applies to the destruction of Samaria. In process of time every detail was fulfilled, but Jerusalem had to be destroyed three times and Samaria twice before that was achieved.

Micah is too long to write out in full, so I would ask readers to have the book open in front of them. The English translation I have used is the *ESV*, the English Standard Version.

****

Structure of Micah

Structure of Micah

A 1:1. The Lord's word to Micah ("Who is like the Lord?")

   B 1:2-16. The Lord is revealed in majesty and judgment

      C 2:1-13. Woe to those who devise wickedness

         D 3:1-12. Hear, you heads of Jacob. Heads and prophets condemned.
            Jerusalem a heap of ruins

           E 4:1-5:15. What will happen in the latter days

         D 6:1-16. Hear what the Lord says. The Lord contends with Israel.
            Jerusalem a desolation and a hissing

      C 7:1-7. Alas to me! The godly has perished from the earth

   B 7:8-17. I will show them marvellous things. The nations cringe in dread

A 7:18-20. Who is like God? The Lord's oath to Abraham and Jacob

Structure of Chapters 4-5 (E above)

A 4:1-5. The latter days. Peoples and nations in peace and security

   B 4:6-7. In that day, declares the Lord, I will assemble the lame … and reign over them in Mount Zion

      C 4:8. And you, O Tower of the Flock. Kingship for Jerusalem

         D 4:9-10. Now why do you cry aloud? No king, exile to Babylon

            E 4:11-13. Now many nations are assembled against you. You will beat them in pieces

         D 5:1. Now muster your troops. Siege is laid, the judge of Israel is struck on the cheek

      C 5:2-6. And you, O Bethlehem Ephrathah. The One to be ruler in Israel. He will deliver us from the Assyrian

A 5:7-9. Peoples and nations torn to pieces by the lion-like remnant of Jacob

   B 5:10-15. In that day, declares the Lord. I will cut off, root out, destroy

The Prophecy of Micah

The Prophecy of Micah

Micah 1:1. Micah of Moresheth

This opening verse has already been mentioned in the Introduction. Like Amos and Habakkuk, Micah not only heard but *saw* the word of the Lord. It was that vivid to him that he could actually see taking place before his eyes the scenes of judgment and deliverance he was about to predict. He prophesied concerning Samaria and Jerusalem. He had a severe message for Samaria in the opening verses, but the rest of the book seems to be addressed by and large to Judah and Jerusalem. Hence only the kings of Judah are mentioned in this verse, not Pekah and Hoshea the corresponding kings in Israel.

1:2-4. Hear, you peoples, all of you

When the Lord speaks everyone is required to listen (Isaiah 1:2; Deut. 32:1). His word may be directed toward some specific nation or people, but it is not confined to that audience. People everywhere should take warning from what is said, since potentially it applies to them as well. His word is a witness "against *you*", not Israel only but "you peoples". They should all pay heed since it may be their turn next, for they too are infected with the same incriminating cancer which is eating away at the vital organs of the body politic.

When the Lord comes out of His place (to punish the inhabitants of the earth for their iniquity, Isaiah 26:21), and treads upon the high places of the earth, cataclysmic upheavals in the realm of nature are to be expected. The mountains will melt under Him (Psalm 97:5), and the valleys will split open like wax before the fire as when waters pour down a steep place. These are the physical manifestations of His coming in judgment as described in many places (e.g. Judges 5:4-5; 2 Samuel 22:8-16; Psalm 97:3-5; Amos 1:2; Habakkuk 3:3-15; Nahum 1:3-6). It is not clear however to what extent they were literally fulfilled at the time of Assyria's invasion of Samaria and Judah.

1:5-7. I will make Samaria a heap in the open country

The objects of the Lord's wrath are Samaria and Jerusalem as explicitly stated in verse 5. For her transgression Samaria would be destroyed (as described in verse 6), and for her sins Judah also would be invaded. Judah would be overrun to the very gates of Jerusalem (9,12). The towns of the Shephelah would be overwhelmed and their inhabitants carried off into exile (16), but on this occasion Jerusalem itself would escape.

This is exactly what happened in the sixth and fourteenth years of Hezekiah. Samaria was destroyed in his sixth year by Sargon king of Assyria, and Judah was invaded eight years later by Sennacherib (716 and 708 BC by my dating). Jerusalem however was miraculously delivered when 185,000 Assyrians were struck down by the angel of the Lord (Isaiah 37:36). Sennacherib departed in haste and Jerusalem was spared.

Other prophets predict the downfall of Samaria, notably Isaiah 28:1-4 ("the proud crown of the drunkards of Ephraim will be trodden underfoot"); Hosea 1:4 ("I will put an end to the kingdom of the house of Israel"); 2:10-12; 10:5-10 ("Samaria's king shall perish"); 13:16 ("Samaria shall bear her guilt because she has rebelled against her God; they shall fall by the sword"); Amos 6:1-8 ("I abhor the pride of Jacob and hate his strongholds, and I will deliver up the city and all that is in it"). Amos spoke against both Zion and the mountain of Samaria, but none of them did so in such explicit terms as Micah.

According to Micah, "I (the Lord) will make Samaria a heap in the open country, a place for planting vineyards, and I will pour down her stones into the valley and uncover her foundations." The word translated "heap" is used of Jerusalem in 3:12 (and Psalm 79:1) while a similar word is used of Damascus in Isaiah 17:1. It means a heap of ruins. Even Samaria's foundations would be torn up and exposed.

Samaria was captured by the Assyrians after a siege of three years in the ninth year of Hoshea and the sixth of Hezekiah (2 Kings 17:6; 18:9-12). This was the immediate fulfilment of Micah's prediction. It happened soon after Micah's warning and was decisive so far as the Northern Kingdom was concerned. That kingdom came to an abrupt end and was never restored. It is not certain however that Samaria was totally destroyed on this occasion; in fact Sargon states in his Annals, "I restored and made it more habitable than before." Samaria was still inhabited by Israelites after the fall of Jerusalem (Jeremiah 41:5) and was an administrative district under the Persians (Ezra 4:10).

The complete fulfilment of Micah's prophecy seems to have occurred in about 110 BC, when the city was captured by John Hyrcanus son of Simon Maccabaeus. He was apparently greatly displeased with the Samaritans for the injuries they had done to the people of Marissa, a colony of the Jews. God was also displeased it would seem seeing that He allowed Hyrcanus to destroy Samaria more thoroughly than ever before. These are the words of Josephus:

> And so Hyrcanus captured the city after besieging it for a year, but not being content with that alone, he effaced it entirely and left it to be swept away by the mountain-torrents, for he dug beneath it until it fell into the beds of the torrents, and so removed all signs of its ever having been a city (*Antiquities* XIII.10.3).

Samaria was partially restored by Pompey and Gabinius, but it was left to Herod to complete its reconstruction in 30 BC. He refortified the city with larger, stronger walls, built a magnificent temple to Rome and Augustus, and renamed it Sebaste (=Augusta) in honour of his patron the Emperor. This marked the end of Samaria as such, for the name Sebaste has clung to it ever since. Even today it is Sebastiyeh on the West Bank.

In this way Micah's prediction was fulfilled by stages until the last detail was in place. The same cumulative fulfilment is evident in the case of Micah 3:12, his prophecy concerning Jerusalem, as we shall see in a moment.

1:8-9. Micah's grief

Micah is overcome with grief at the terrible fate awaiting Samaria. He had after all *seen* it (1:1) enacted before his very eyes, not simply been told about it. He was all the more grief-stricken because Samaria's incurable wound had come to Judah; it had reached to the very gate of Micah's people, to Jerusalem (1:9). His own people, even his own town of Moresheth-gath, now lay in the path of the invading Assyrians.

He says, "I will go stripped and naked", but the consonantal text says "plundered" rather than stripped. The Masoretes have corrected the written text but without good reason. "Micah's intention", says Keil, "is not only to exhibit publicly his mourning for the approaching calamity of Judah, but also to set forth in a symbolic form the fate that awaits the Judeans."[3] Even if the translation "stripped" is retained the meaning is not significantly altered. This is precisely what Isaiah did for three whole years to show forth the fate awaiting Egypt and Cush (Isaiah 20).

Jackals and ostriches are doleful creatures inhabiting the desert and lonely places. They both make a piteous, howling noise sometimes mistaken for women and children.

1:10-16. Disaster from the Lord to the gate of Jerusalem

The fate of twelve cities ranging from Gath to Jerusalem is here described in pictorial language replete with alliteration and word-play. He begins with the well-known words from David's lament over Saul and Jonathan in 2 Samuel 1:20, "Tell it not in Gath!"

The sixth city named *after* Gath is Lachish, a large fortress city on the western edge of the Judean lowlands, the Shephelah. According to Mays[4], the cities after Lachish are spaced in an arc about twelve miles in length, curving away north-east into the Shephelah, all in close proximity. Most of the place-names before Lachish are unidentified, but judging from the likely location of Beth-le-aphrah, "the cities named before Lachish lie to the south-east running up into the hill country and not reaching beyond a distance of twelve to fifteen miles."

---

[3] Carl F Kiel, *The Twelve Minor Prophets,* Erdman's edition, Vol. 1, p. 430.
[4] Mays, pp. 52-53.

It was from this direction that Sennacherib invaded Judah in the fourteenth year of Hezekiah. It was from Lachish that he dispatched a large army to Hezekiah at Jerusalem (2 Kings 18:17). The siege of Lachish is displayed in relief on the walls of his palace. Lachish he captured, but Jerusalem he did not as his silence bears witness. This invasion reached to the gates of Jerusalem, but Jerusalem itself was spared as we know from the detailed accounts in 2 Kings 18-19, 2 Chronicles 32 and Isaiah 36-37.

Beth-le-aphrah, the house of dust, is told to roll in the dust as an expression of sorrow and mourning. Shaphir, beautiful, is told to go its way in shameful nakedness, the opposite of beauty. Zaanan, one who goes out (to battle), will not go out. Beth-ezel, the one who stands by another, will lose its own standing-place. Maroth, bitterness, waits anxiously for good, but only evil comes. Lachish is told to harness the steeds (*la-rechesh*) to the chariots. Moresheth-gath, Micah's birthplace meaning "possession of Gath", will receive parting gifts. Achzib will prove a deceitful brook (*achzab*), one that dries up when needed most, to the kings of Israel. A possessor (*yoresh*) will the Lord bring against Mareshah, possession. To Adullam where David escaped from Saul, the glory of Israel (her wealth and nobles) will flee for refuge. They are told to make themselves bald and to cut off their hair because Israel's pampered children ("the children of your delight") are going into exile.

2:1-5. Woe to those who devise wickedness

The gist of this passage is clear. The rich landowners were adding field to field, house to house, at the expense of the poor farmer who was robbed of his property and livelihood (so also Isaiah 5:8). The landowners had the power to do it; it was in the power of their hands because the system allowed it through corruption and bribery.

They devised evil schemes on their beds at night and carried them out as soon as morning light permitted. They coveted fields and seized them, houses and took them. For this evil they could expect to be recompensed in kind. They were not the only ones to *devise evil*; the Lord was also devising evil from which they could not escape. The fields which they had seized would be taken from them and allotted to an 'apostate'. Because they had robbed men of their inheritance, they would themselves have no-one to cast the line by lot in the assembly of the Lord.

2:6-11. Micah is told to shut up

Like other prophets before him (Amos 2:12; 7:12-13), Micah is told to shut up. Literally, "Do not drip, they drip, you should not drip about these things. Disgrace will not overtake us." It sounds highly insulting and may be so. Amos was also told, "Do not prophesy against Israel, and do not *drip* against the house of Isaac" (7:16). In Ezekiel 21:2 however the prophet is told by the Lord to set his face toward Jerusalem and "*drip* against the sanctuaries, and prophesy against the land of Israel." It is probable therefore that drip is just another word for preach without any pejorative intentions.

In reply Micah insists that God's patience is not yet exhausted and that His words do good to those who walk uprightly. He then hurls more incrimination at them. Men who pass by trustingly they strip of their robes, women they drive from their pleasant houses, and even little children are deprived of "my splendour" for ever, meaning perhaps their inheritance in the land which gave them dignity or their God-given self-respect as free citizens and true Israelites.

His final thrust returns to the subject of prophesying. The only sort of preacher (dripper) these people deserved was one who uttered wind and lies and preached (dripped) about wine and strong drink! He would be the preacher for these people!

2:12-13. The remnant of Israel will be gathered like sheep in a fold

The concluding verses of chapter 2 give reassurance to "the remnant of Israel". It is implied that the nation would be reduced to a remnant by the impending invasion. Their place of exile is compared to a prison with walls and gates. These must be broken through to effect their release. The one who opens the breach and leads them out is Jehovah their King. He will go before them as at the Exodus when "the Lord went before them by day in a pillar of cloud … and by night in a pillar of fire" (Exodus 13:21).

One might compare Jeremiah 23:3, "Then I will gather the remnant of my flock out of all the countries where I have driven them, and I will bring them back to their fold", or Micah 4:6-7.

In verse 12 "all of you, O Jacob" is equated with "the remnant of Israel". So when the Bible says that "all Israel will be saved" (Romans 11:26), we are not to think of every Israelite, but the Israel of God, the believing remnant. The remnant idea is very important to Micah (see 4:7; 5:7; 7:18). This he has in common with Isaiah who has a lot to say about the remnant (10:20-23; 11:11,16).

3:1-4. You eat the flesh of my people

In these verses the heads and rulers of Israel are addressed, and it is primarily the perversion of justice which Micah has against them. In Exodus 18:25 Moses chose able men and made them *heads* over the people. Their function was to administer justice. In Judges 11:11 Jephthah was made by the people "head and leader" over them, using the same words as in Micah 3:1. The word "leader" is also used by Isaiah for officials in Jerusalem (1:10; 3:6,7; 22:3).

In Micah they are compared to cannibals who tear the skin off the people and eat their flesh. Like butchers they take off the skin, break up the bones, chop up the meat, and boil the flesh in the cauldron. They know nothing about justice, these haters of good and lovers of evil. When in their extremity they cry to the Lord, He will pay no attention to them "because they have made their deeds evil."

3:5-8. The prophets lead my people astray

Micah next points his finger at the prophets who lead the people astray. What comes out of their mouths depends entirely on what goes in! If they are given something to eat, they prophesy peace; if given nothing they wage a holy war against them. To "sanctify war" sounds like a jihad (as in Jeremiah 6:4 and Joel 3:9), but in this instance a personal vendetta.

The prophets will receive their just reward for prophesying lies. "The seers shall be disgraced, and the diviners put to shame." There will be no word from the Lord when the sun goes down on these prophets. But Micah himself is in a different league altogether. "But as for me," he says, "I am filled with power, with the spirit of the Lord, and with justice and might, to declare to Jacob his transgression and to Israel his sin."

3:9-11. They build Zion with blood and Jerusalem with iniquity

In these verses he turns again on the heads and rulers, those whose job was to administer justice. These judges detest justice; instead of making things straight, they make crooked all that is straight. They build Zion with blood and Jerusalem with iniquity. Habakkuk makes the same accusation but his words are directed against the proud Chaldeans: "Woe to him who builds a town with blood and founds a city on iniquity!" (2:12)

The love of money is the driving force for Israel's corrupt leaders. The heads, priests and prophets were no different in this respect. Their services (for what they were worth) were available only to those who paid the most. But they still had the audacity to say, "Is not the Lord in the midst of us? No disaster shall come upon us." Micah however was about to disillusion them! He had a very different message to convey.

3:12. Jerusalem to become a heap of ruins

"Therefore because of you Zion shall be ploughed as a field; Jerusalem shall become a heap of ruins, and the mountain of the house a wooded height." In the words of Keil, "The royal palace, the city, and the temple shall be so utterly destroyed, that of all the houses and palaces only heaps of rubbish will remain, and the ground upon which the city stood will be partly used as a ploughed field and partly overgrown with bushes."[5]

---

[5] Keil, pp. 454-55.

And all this was to happen "because of you", the corrupt heads, priests and prophets of Micah's day. It should therefore have taken place in the reign of Hezekiah. The judgment described in chapter 1 had already been fulfilled in the sixth and fourteenth years of Hezekiah. Samaria had been sacked and Judah invaded up to the gates of Jerusalem. Jerusalem was spared in Hezekiah's fourteenth year, but now a far worse judgment is predicted. This must have been uttered later in Hezekiah's reign as Judah's moral decline plummeted to levels previously unheard of. Judah was now in terminal decline in spite of Hezekiah's best endeavours to stem the ebbing tide.

There was however a temporary reprieve. Because Hezekiah humbled himself and entreated the Lord, the Lord relented of the disaster that He had pronounced against them (Jeremiah 26:19). It did not happen in Micah's day, but a hundred years later Jeremiah made a similar prophecy in the Lord's name. "I will make this house like Shiloh, and I will make this city a curse for all the nations of the earth" (26:6). For daring to predict the desolation of the city and Temple Jeremiah was condemned to death by the priests and prophets, but the officials and all the people intervened on his behalf. They pointed out that Micah had not been put to death for predicting the desolation of Jerusalem. Hezekiah had entreated the Lord and the disaster had been averted.

Here we have an excellent example of postponed fulfilment. The Israelites were familiar with this principle. They knew the Lord was merciful and forgiving. As Pusey says, "He spoke to those who knew that God pardoned on repentance, who had lately had before them that marvellous instance in Nineveh." (See the book of Jonah.)

It was not until 586 BC that Jerusalem fell prey to the Babylonian invader. This was in fulfilment of Micah's prophecy as much as Jeremiah's repeated warnings. The damage then inflicted on the stricken city was certainly extensive. Jeremiah speaks of jackals prowling over the desolate city (Lamentations 5:18). There is no evidence however that Zion was ploughed as a field, as foretold by Micah.

The city was finally and totally destroyed by the Romans in AD 70. With the exception of three towers which were deliberately left standing, "the city was so completely levelled to the ground as to leave future visitors to the spot no ground for believing that it had ever been inhabited" (Josephus, *Wars* VII.1.1). Terentius Rufus, who was left in command of the Roman army, did at that time tear up the foundations of the Temple with a ploughshare. Still, Micah's prophecy was to receive a more remarkable fulfilment. This occurred in AD 135 after the Bar-Cochba revolt. I quote again from Pusey:

> At this time there appears to have been a formal act, whereby the Romans marked the legal annihilation of cities; an act esteemed, at this time, one of most extreme severity. When a city was to be built, its compass was marked with a plough; the Romans, where they willed to unmake a city, did, on rare occasions, turn up its soil with a plough. Hence the saying, "A city with a plough is built, with a plough overthrown". The city so ploughed forfeited all civil rights; it was counted to have ceased to be.[6]

Thus was Jerusalem ploughed as a field in AD 135 on the orders of the emperor Aelius Hadrianus. When, shortly after, the city was rebuilt, it was given, like Samaria before it, a pagan name. It

---

[6] E.B. Pusey, *The Minor Prophets*, 1860, at Micah 3:12.

was called Aelia after the emperor Hadrian. Here we have another example of the cumulative fulfilment of prophecy. Doubtless other examples could be given where predictions of woe against cities or nations were fulfilled by stages over a period of centuries.

4:1-5. Out of Zion shall go forth the law

Micah 4-5 forms an extended section of the book relating to "the end of days". It is however closely connected with what precedes. Micah 3:12 spoke of the mountain of the house becoming a wooded height; in 4:1 he has a very different role for "the mountain of the house of the Lord". It would now be established as the highest of the mountains with peoples and nations flowing there!

It might have happened in a comparatively short space of time. The fall of Jerusalem would be followed by exile to Babylon (4:10), and from Babylon they would be rescued and redeemed from the grip of their enemies. This would be accomplished by none other than their Messiah who would have been born and brought up in Bethlehem during the intervening years (5:1-4). Micah's programme is in essence the same as that more fully elaborated in the later chapters of Isaiah and in Jeremiah.

Verses 1-3 of chapter 4 are the same as in Isaiah 2:2-4. In Micah they are neatly interlocked with the last verse of chapter 3 and also with what follows whereas in Isaiah they stand on their own. It is likely therefore that they were first revealed to Micah and that Isaiah repeated them under the Lord's direction.

Micah 4:1 tells us that "the mountain of the house of the Lord shall be established as the highest of the mountains; it shall be lifted up above the hills, and peoples shall flow to it." It was impossible for the mountain of the house to remain a ruin; its glorious future is here revealed, no longer simply the mountain of the house, but now the mountain of the house *of the Lord.*"

The Temple mount will become the highest of the mountains. It will be physically lifted up by the massive earthquake which will split the city in two at the return of Christ (Zechariah 14:4). The surrounding country will be turned into a plain from Geba to Rimmon, but Jerusalem shall remain aloft on its site (14:10). Geba was in Benjamin about six miles north-east of Jerusalem; Rimmon (En-Rimmon) 33 miles south-west of Jerusalem. With the flattening of this entire area Jerusalem will dominate the scene. "Great is the Lord and greatly to be praised in the city of our God! His holy mountain, beautiful in elevation, is the joy of all the earth, Mount Zion, in the far north, the city of the great King" (Psalm 48:1-2).

Zion, thus elevated, will exercise a magnetic attraction for all the nations. They will not come as sightseers to admire its beauty, but to receive instruction in the ways of the Lord and the right path to take. "For out of Zion shall go forth the law, and the word of the Lord from Jerusalem" (Isaiah 2:3). Nations and peoples will flow into it in a never-ending stream, simply to receive instruction and to hear the word of the Lord. "In that day there will be a highway from Egypt to Assyria ... and the Egyptians will worship with the Assyrians" (Isaiah 19:23). They will come to Jerusalem to worship the King.

The Lord will judge between many peoples and decide for strong nations. He will arbitrate over their disputes and adjudicate in all matters of international concern. The nations will enthusiastically go along with whatever is decided. War will be a thing of the past; it will not even be taught any more. Instead they will occupy themselves in peaceful and profitable pursuits which will generate domestic bliss and prosperity in every area of existence. They will sit every man under his vine and fig-tree in safety and security, as was the case to a lesser degree and far shorter time during the peaceful reign of Solomon (1 Kings 4:25).

All this however will not be achieved without an enormous struggle. The nations will have to be disciplined, brought to heel, and purged of rebels. This will be a painful process accomplished by the Lord with the help of His converted people (see 5:7-15).

4:6-7. The lame and rejected will become a strong nation

At that time the Lord will assemble and gather those who have been driven away and afflicted. This company (those remaining after the destruction of Jerusalem and the dispersion of Israel's population) He will turn into the remnant, and those who were cast off into a strong nation.

Here we meet with the remnant again (see 2:12). It is they who will become the strong nation over whom the Lord will reign in Mount Zion. This verse is similar to Zephaniah 3:19 where the words *lame* and *driven away* are found again. "Behold, at that time I will deal with all your oppressors. And I will save the lame and gather the outcast (driven away), and I will change their shame into praise and renown in all the earth."

These two passages contain three of the four occurrences of lame (Hebrew *tsala*) in the Old Testament. The fourth is found in Genesis 32:31 where we read that Jacob was lame because of his hip. This was after he had wrestled with the Lord and prevailed, and his name was changed from Jacob to Israel. The new Israel, the converted Israel of the future, will be composed of those who have wrestled with the Lord and prevailed. They are the lame and the outcast whom the Lord will make into a strong nation in the same way as lame Jacob became a nation numerous and strong. He will take away their shame and make them "a name" in all the earth (Zephaniah 3:19).

4:8. And you, O tower of the flock

"And you, O tower of the flock (Eder), hill (Ophel) of the daughter of Zion, to you shall it come, the former dominion shall come, kingship for the daughter of Jerusalem." This verse corresponds to 5:2-4, "And you, O Bethlehem Ephrathah … from you shall come forth for me one who is to be ruler in Israel."

The phrase Tower of Eder (or Flock-tower) is found again only in Genesis 35:21. Jacob was travelling from Bethel, twelve miles north of Jerusalem, toward Ephrath (later called Bethlehem) six miles south of Jerusalem. On the way Rachel died giving birth to Benjamin and was buried on the way to Ephrath (that is Bethlehem). Israel (Jacob) then journeyed on and pitched his tent beyond the Tower of Eder. We are thinking therefore of a shepherd's watchtower not far from Bethlehem.

In Micah the Tower of Eder is identified with Ophel, David's hill in Jerusalem (Mount Zion). This veiled reference to Bethlehem and its vicinity is taken up in 5:2-4 where we discover that Israel's future Ruler will be born at Bethlehem Ephrathah.

4:9-10. You shall go to Babylon and there you shall be rescued

The prophet now reverts, as is his custom, to Judah's grief and pain when their king and city would be captured and they themselves, Judah's populace, go out from the city, dwell in the open country and be carried off to Babylon. Judah's distress at this time of reckoning is compared to that of a woman in labour, a comparison which Jeremiah makes use of repeatedly (4:31; 6:24; 13:21 etc.).

Keil[7] is doubtless correct in saying that the mention of Babylon as the place of exile "goes so far beyond the bounds of the political horizon of Micah's time, that it cannot be accounted for from any natural presentiment." Assyria was then the scourge of that part of the world, and it was Assyria of course who captured Samaria in 716 (my date!) and invaded Judah in 708. Isaiah however had already warned Hezekiah, after the visit of envoys from Merodach-baladan king of Babylon, that everything in his house would be carried off to Babylon and that even some of his sons "shall be taken away and they shall be eunuchs in the palace of the king of Babylon" (Isaiah 39:5-7). And in the later chapters of Isaiah Babylon is the place of exile (43:14; 47:6; 48:20).

Micah gives expression to the same unpopular (and at that time improbable) prediction that Jerusalem's future conqueror would be Babylon and that to Babylon the exiles would go. He does however conclude on a happier note: "There you shall be rescued; there the Lord will redeem you from the hand of your enemies."

4:11-13. Many nations are assembled against you

This is the second of three sections beginning with "Now" (see 4:9 and 5:1). As he peers into the future Micah finds his vision focusing on yet another invasion. Again "many nations" are involved (see 4:2) but this time they are intent on destroying Jerusalem. "Let her be defiled," they say, "and let our eyes gaze

---

[7] Keil, p. 466.

upon Zion." They want to feast their eyes on the city thus defiled and profaned, to gaze on her intently, to gloat (*NIV*).

This is not the same invasion as that already described when the people are taken captive to Babylon. On this second occasion the invading nations are pulverized by the daughter of Zion who is supernaturally energized to thresh the nations like sheaves on the threshing-floor. "Arise and thresh, O daughter of Zion, for I will make your horn iron, and I will make your hoofs bronze; you shall beat in pieces many peoples." The same advice is given in Joel 3:13 and Revelation 14:14-20, referring to the same event. Iron and bronze were proverbial for their strength. So Jeremiah asks, "Can one break iron, iron from the north and bronze?" (15:12). What better weapon for breaking in pieces than something that cannot itself be broken?

Keil[8] comes near to the truth when he says, "We must therefore understand these verses as referring to the events already predicted by Joel (ch.3), and afterwards by Ezekiel (38-39) and Zechariah (12), and in Rev.20:8 ff, i.e. to the last great attack which the nations of the world will make upon the church of the Lord, that has been redeemed from Babel."

But Keil is mistaken in thinking that Revelation 20:8-9 refers to the same event. Though of a similar nature and intent, that invasion takes place "when the thousand years are ended". He is also wrong in getting the church involved. This invasion is directed against Zion (4:11), the land of unwalled villages (Ezek. 38:11), Jerusalem (Zech. 12:3,9); and the battle takes place in the valley of Jehoshaphat (Joel 3:12), between the Sea and the glorious holy mountain (Daniel 11:45). It will take place immediately before the return of Christ, and He will be the true

---

[8] Keil, p. 474.

victor using Israel as His battleaxe (Micah 5:5; Zech. 12:7-9; 14:3-4).

5:1. With a rod they strike the judge of Israel

This verse, which also begins with "Now", reverts to the siege which Micah was anticipating in the near future. He had already said, "Is there no king in you? Has your counsellor perished?" (4:9). He now says, "with a rod they strike the judge of Israel on the cheek." Either the same person is meant by king, counsellor and judge, or high-ranking officials in different departments. To strike someone on the cheek was an act of contempt and provocation (1 Kings 22:24; Job 16:10; Psalm 3:7; Lam. 3:30; Matt. 5:39; Acts 23:2).

Mays[9] translates the first clause, "Now gash yourself, daughter of marauders!" To gash is indeed the more usual meaning of the verb, but both the sense and the alliteration (*hithgodedu bath-gedud*) confirm the translation, "Now muster your troops, O daughter of troops." This is the meaning of the verb in Jeremiah 5:7. Micah speaks of a siege. The siege is followed by the destruction of Jerusalem (3:12), and that is followed by exile to Babylon (4:10). All this took place between the ninth and eleventh years of Zedekiah, 589-586 BC (2 Kings 25; Jeremiah 39).

5:2-4. Bethlehem Ephrathah, from you shall come forth...

The birth of the "Deliverer" in Bethlehem Ephrathah is mentioned in close connection with the siege of Jerusalem and the humiliation of Israel's ruler. Israel would be given up, but only until such time as "she who is in labour has given birth" (5:3). At

---

[9] Mays, p. 111.

that time also "the rest of his brothers shall return to the people of Israel."

A situation is envisaged in which some of the nation are still in the land when the Christ is born in Bethlehem Ephrathah. The rest of his brothers will return home as a result of His birth and subsequent rule. He will stand and shepherd His flock in the strength of the Lord, and they will dwell in complete security, "for he shall be great to the ends of the earth, and he shall be their peace."

Bethlehem Ephrathah is designated as the birthplace of the coming Ruler. Ephrath, meaning fruitful, was the earlier name for Bethlehem, and is identified with Bethlehem in Genesis 35:19 and 48:7. Both Jesse, David's father, and Elimelech, Ruth's father-in-law, are described as Ephrathites from Bethlehem in Judah (1 Samuel 17:12; Ruth 1:2). Bethlehem is here said to be "too little to be among the clans of Judah." Similar words are used of Saul's and Gideon's families in 1 Samuel 9:21 and Judges 6:15. From this insignificant village would come forth the One who would be Ruler in Israel, whose goings forth were from of old, from ancient days. With these words compare Proverbs 8:22-23 where Wisdom personified is none other than the pre-incarnate Christ.

Keil[10] correctly says, "The birth of the Messiah in Bethlehem, and not in Jerusalem the city of David, presupposes that the family of David, out of which it is to spring, will have lost the throne, and have fallen into poverty. This could only arise from the giving up of Israel into the power of its enemies." It was of course from Bethlehem that David's family originated, his father Jesse being a Bethlehemite (1 Samuel 16).

---

[10] Keil, p. 483.

The duration of Israel's exile in Babylon is not specified in Micah nor even in Isaiah. In Jeremiah however it is limited to seventy years. Before the end of this period Messiah should have grown to manhood according to both Micah and Isaiah. He would also be "wounded for our transgressions" and "prolong his days" before Israel's restoration according to Isaiah 53. This forecast was subsequently withdrawn and postponed, but Christ was still born in Bethlehem while the majority of His countrymen were living in exile (as they still are) in various parts of the world. At that time many of them were still in Babylon (1 Peter 5:13, "The [diaspora] in Babylon sends you greetings"). In the future also Babylon the great will hold the Lord's people in its thrall and will persecute and kill many of them (Revelation 18:4,24). They are commanded, "Come out of her, my people, lest you take part in her sins, lest you share in her plagues."

The chief priests and scribes knew that the Christ would be born in Bethlehem (Matthew 2:1-6), but the news of His birth conveyed by the wise men does not seem to have moved them. Not a single one volunteered to accompany the wise men to Bethlehem. They probably regarded the Magi as Gentile charlatans whose star-gazing was a symptom of their pagan blindness (Isaiah 47:13). They knew the letter of the Old Testament, but the letter kills unless the Spirit gives life (2 Corinthians 3:6).

5:5-6. He will deliver us from the Assyrian

Verse 5 begins with the words, "And he shall be their peace." But how will this be achieved? The answer is given in verses 5-6. "When the Assyrian comes into our land and treads in our palaces, then we will raise against him seven shepherds and eight princes of men; they shall shepherd the land of Assyria with the sword, and the land of Nimrod at its entrances; and **He** shall deliver us from the Assyrian..."

The Assyrian (*Ashur*, Assyria) is synonymous with the many nations of Micah 4:11. He is so called because Assyria was Israel's scourge in the reigns of Ahaz and Hezekiah, and the name is carried over to describe Israel's final invader who will occupy the same territory and invade from the same direction. It is especially Isaiah who speaks of the invader in these terms. In Isaiah 10:24-34 it is said, "the Lord of hosts will wield against them a whip, as when he struck Midian at the rock of Oreb."

In 14:25 the Lord gives His word, "I will break the Assyrian in my land, and on my mountains trample him underfoot." In 30:29-33 the destruction of the Assyrian is executed "in furious anger and a flame of devouring fire, with a cloudburst and storm and hailstones." The Assyrians will be terror-stricken at the voice of the Lord when He strikes with His rod. In 31:8-9 the Assyrian falls by the sword, "a sword, not of man, shall devour him." But the most graphic account of all is given in Zechariah 12.

Micah takes up the same theme. When the Assyrian has the temerity to tread within Israel's borders and to trample on her palaces, the Lord will raise up "shepherds" who will "shepherd the land of Assyria with the sword, and the land of Nimrod in its gates (or, with drawn sword, *NIV*)." Nimrod was the founder of both Babylon and Nineveh (Genesis 10:10-11). It is as founder of Assyria that he is here referred to.

5:7-9. The remnant of Jacob like a lion among the sheep

These verses return to the subject of many peoples and nations. In 4:1-4 they were seen streaming up to Jerusalem to receive instruction and arbitration, beating their swords into ploughshares and dwelling securely under their vines and fig-trees. In 5:7-9 a twofold picture is presented. On the one hand the remnant of Jacob act like dew from the Lord, like showers on the grass, in the midst of many peoples. Their actions and influence are altogether benevolent and beneficial. But on the other hand, they will fall on the nations "like a lion among the beasts of the forest, like a young lion among the flocks of sheep." Among these they tread down and tear in pieces.

Clearly two kinds of nations are in view, on the one hand the compliant and obedient whom the Lord is able to nurture and instruct; on the other hand the stubborn and rebellious who have to be brought to heel. In due course righteousness and reason will prevail and the idyllic conditions of Micah 4:1-4 will flourish throughout the world.

5:10-15. I will cut off, root out, and destroy

These verses begin in the same way as 4:6-7: "And in the day, declares the Lord". There we were told about the lame, whom the Lord would make the remnant and a strong nation, over which He would reign in Mount Zion for evermore. In the present verses we hear the other side of the story: the eradication of everything offensive to the Lord. These include horses, chariots, cities, strongholds, sorceries, fortune-tellers, carved images, pillars, idols and Asherahs, everything in fact in which the people were tempted to trust and rely on, everything which turned their hearts away from the Lord.

In the law also the verb "cut off" is used of a wide variety of offences. What is here said of Israel applies as well to the nations that do not obey.

6:1-5. How have I wearied you? Answer me!

The Lord has a case to plead, an indictment against His people Israel, and He calls upon the mountains, hills and the foundations of the earth to bear witness to what He has to say. On occasions of great solemnity it was not unusual for the Lord to call upon heaven and earth as witnesses (e.g. Deuteronomy 4:26; 30:19; 31:28).

The question He puts to them is this: "O my people, what have I done to you? How have I wearied you? Answer me!" He then reminds them of the innumerable "saving acts" which He had done on their behalf: how He had brought them out of Egypt, redeeming them from the house of slavery; how He had sent them Moses, Aaron and Miriam; how Balak king of Moab had planned evil against Israel but was thwarted by Balaam's response in blessing them repeatedly; and how He had led them into the promised land all the way from Shittim to Gilgal. Shittim was the last place of encampment beyond Jordan and Gilgal their first encampment in Canaan.

What complaint could the Israelites possibly have when He had acted towards them so graciously and for such a long time?

6:6-8. Will the Lord be pleased with thousands of rams?

The people are not so much ashamed as mystified by these words, assuming their reply is basically sincere. "What more do you expect of us?" they seem to be saying. Is it more burnt offerings you require? How many thousands of rams will you find acceptable, how many rivers of oil? Shall I offer my firstborn son for my transgression, the fruit of my body for the sin of my soul? Is that what you require?

They may have genuinely thought that offering up their firstborn son was the ultimate sacrifice which would move the Lord to look favourably on their plight. Ahaz, Hezekiah's father, had burned his sons as an offering in accordance with the abominations of the heathen (2 Chronicles 28:3), and his son Manasseh did the same (33:6). Hezekiah made a clean sweep of all such heathen practices, but they may have lingered on in spite of his reforms or crept back later in his reign.

It is of the essence of man-made religion to imagine that God is won over or appeased by acts involving huge personal sacrifice or self-denial. But what He is really looking for is an attitude which expresses itself in acts of kindness, justice, decency and humility, as stated in verse 8. "He has told you, O man, what is good; and what does the Lord require of you but to do justice, and to love kindness, and to walk humbly with your God?"

They had been told this back in Deuteronomy 10:12, "And now, Israel, what does the Lord your God require of you, but to fear the Lord your God, to walk in all his ways, to love him, to serve the Lord your God with all your heart and all your soul..." This is the message of all the prophets and of the New Testament as well. James has this to say, "Religion that is pure and undefiled before God, the Father, is this: to visit orphans and widows in their affliction, and to keep oneself unstained from the world" (1:27).

The Israelites of Micah's day were hell-bent on every dishonest practice known to man. Offering up thousands of rams, or even their own children, was a small price to pay so long as they could go on defrauding and abusing their fellow Israelite as they had grown accustomed to doing.

6:9-12. Can I forget any longer the scant measure that is accursed?

So far from doing justice and acts of loving-kindness, the rich Israelites had no thought or concern whatsoever for the welfare (or even survival) of their poor neighbours. The scant measure, the dishonest scales, the bag of deceitful weights were for them everyday practice. They would even stoop to violence and lies to get their own way.

Their practices contravened the clear directives of the law, not to mention the law universal written on men's hearts (Romans 2:15). They should have been familiar with Deuteronomy 25:13-16. "You shall not have in your bag two kinds of weights, a large and a small. You shall not have in your house two kinds of measures, a large and a small. A full and fair weight you shall have, a full and fair measure you shall have, that your days may be long in the land that the Lord your God is giving you. For all who do such things, all who act dishonestly, are an abomination to the Lord your God."

How could they expect their days to be long in the land when they had failed so lamentably to meet the conditions? If the truth be told their days were now extremely short and few as Micah has now to tell them.

6:13-16. I will make you a desolation and your inhabitants a hissing

Because of their sins they must expect "a grievous blow" which would make them desolate. The evils consequent on disobedience would come upon them with increasing and cumulative force (see Deuteronomy 28:15 ff.). They would eat and not be satisfied, store up but preserve nothing because the marauders would take it. There would be no corn, oil or wine because the harvests would fail. "For you have kept the statutes of Omri, and all the works of the house of Ahab; and you have walked in their counsels."

There was no-one like Ahab who sold himself to do what was evil in the sight of the Lord (1 Kings 21:25). It was he who married Jezebel, daughter of Ethbaal king of the Sidonians. Ahab did more to provoke the Lord than all the kings before him. He built the house of Baal in Samaria, erected there an altar for Baal, and encouraged Baal worship throughout the land (1 Kings 16:29-33). Not so much is known about his father Omri or "the statutes of Omri" mentioned by Micah. But he it was who started it all, and Athaliah who married Jehoram king of Judah is called "the daughter of Omri", her grandfather, in both Kings and Chronicles, rather than daughter of Ahab.

There would be no reprieve for Judah. They would have to pay the ultimate price for their apostasy. "I will make you a desolation (*shammah*) and your inhabitants a hissing (*shereqah*); so shall you bear the scorn (*cherpah*) of my people."

It was revealed to Solomon as soon as he had finished building the Temple that if he or his descendants abandoned the law and worshipped other gods, then "Israel will become a proverb and a byword among all peoples. And this house will become a heap of ruins. Everyone passing by it will be astonished and will hiss, and they will say, 'Why has the Lord done this to this land and to this house?'" (1 Kings 9:7-8).

Jeremiah takes up Micah's warnings in almost identical language. In Jeremiah 19:8 the Lord says, "I will make this city a horror (*shammah*), a thing to be hissed at (*shereqah*). Everyone who passes by it will be horrified, and will hiss because of all its wounds (*makkotheka*, cp. *hakkotheka*, Micah 6:13)". In 29:18 he uses the word *reproach* as well. "I will pursue them with the sword, famine, and pestilence and will make them a horror to all the kingdoms of the world, to be a curse, a terror (*shammah*), a hissing (*shereqah*), and a reproach (*cherpah*) among all nations where I have driven them." See also Jeremiah 25:9 and 18.

The desolation of the land and city is here described as in Micah 3:12 and 6:16. This prophecy was fulfilled in all but a few details between 589 and 586 BC by the armies of Nebuchadnezzar king of Babylon.

7:1-7. The godly has perished from the earth

The words translated "Woe is me!" appear again only in Job 10:15. Job there bewails his plight: "If I am guilty, woe is me! If I am in the right, I cannot lift up my head." That is how Micah feels. He is like a hungry man after all the summer fruit has been gathered in. "There is no cluster to eat, no first-ripe fig that my soul desires."

The metaphor is explained in verse 2. "The godly has perished from the earth, and there is no one upright among mankind." What a bleak situation to be in – no righteous man in the entire world, least of all in Israel.

The only thing they are any good at is doing evil! "They all lie in wait for blood, and each hunts the other with a net. Their hands are on what is evil, to do it well; the prince and the judge ask for a bribe, and the great man utters the (evil) desire of his soul." The desire of Micah's soul was to find an upright man on the earth, but the desire of this man's soul was to rob his poor neighbour of his last penny!

One of the worst aspects of the times was the complete breakdown of family trust and respect. A man's enemies are those of his own household: son against father, daughter against mother, daughter-in-law against mother-in-law, even husband against wife. It was no longer safe even to confide in one's own wife, let alone friend or neighbour.

Micah however looks away to his God where there is salvation both for himself and (ultimately) for Israel as well. "I will look to the Lord; I will wait for the God of my salvation; my God will hear me."

7:8-10. He will bring me out to the light

The contrite people of God, fallen but now humble, confess their confidence in the Lord who will rescue them from the darkness and indignation they are experiencing because of their sin. He will plead their cause, execute judgment on their behalf, and bring them out into the light. All this their enemies will see. It is their turn now to be ashamed and treated with contempt.

Both the speaker and the enemy are represented as feminine. The speaker is Jerusalem, the daughter of Zion, and their enemy is the nations who wish their destruction. It is they who say, "Where is their God?" (see Joel 2:17). Previously they had been saying, "Let our eyes gaze upon Zion" (as in Micah 4:11). Now Israel's eyes will look upon her as she is trampled down like the mire of the streets.

7:11-17. Let them graze in Bashan and Gilead as in the days of old

Excitement grows with the threefold repetition of "day... in that day... in that day." It is that day mentioned in 4:6 when the Lord will assemble the lame and make them into a strong nation; and the day mentioned in 5:10 when the Lord will cut off and throw down everything that offends. It is a day for the building of walls and for making the *hoq* far away. *Hoq* usually means statute, but the meaning here is unclear. It could be the decree of the enemy by which he held her captive (Pusey[11]).

The exiles will return from every quarter of the globe, "from Assyria and the cities of Egypt, and from Egypt to the River (Euphrates), from sea to sea and from mountain to mountain." This joyful occasion is a favourite theme in all the prophets, Egypt and Assyria being mentioned in many of them (e.g. Isaiah 11:11-12; 27:13; Hosea 11:10-11; Zech. 10:8-10). The earth however will be desolate by and large, the consequence of the wicked deeds of the earth's inhabitants. God will punish the nations "for the fruit of their deeds", as Isaiah 24 describes at length.

Verse 14 is a petition to the Lord in His capacity as Israel's Shepherd: "Shepherd your people with your staff, the flock of your inheritance... let them graze in Bashan and Gilead as in the days of old." Bashan and Gilead were fertile pasturelands on the east of the Jordan as was Carmel in the west. Their present condition is one of dwelling alone in a forest in the midst of a garden land (Carmel), the sorry state to which Israel had been reduced. In Isaiah 29:17 is the promise, "Lebanon shall be turned

---

[11] Pusey at Micah 7:11.

into a fruitful field (Carmel), and the fruitful field shall be regarded as a forest." Likewise Isaiah 32:15 and Jeremiah 50:19.

The Lord's answer is given in verses 15-17. "As in the days when you came out of the land of Egypt, I will show them marvellous things", He says. When the nations see the wonderful saving acts of the Lord they will be utterly ashamed. They will be speechless in horror and alarm. They will lick the dust like a serpent in shame and remorse (Psalm 72:9; Isaiah 49:23). They will come trembling out of their strongholds and turn in dread to the Lord God. They will now be in fear of the Jews whom they will regard with awe.

Previously they had been saying, "Let her be defiled, and let our eyes gaze upon Zion." How different will their attitude be when they have been brought to their senses as well as to their knees. Then they will say, "Come, let us go up to the mountain of the Lord, to the house of the God of Jacob, that he may teach us his ways, and that we may walk in his paths" (4:2)!

7:18-20. Who is a God like you, pardoning iniquity?

"Who is a God like you, pardoning iniquity and passing over transgression for the remnant of his inheritance?" It is not of course only for the remnant of Israel that He pardons iniquity and passes over transgression. He does that for all His people. "He will tread *our* iniquities under foot. *You* will cast all our sins into the depths of the sea."

He cannot but show faithfulness to Jacob and steadfast love to Abraham because He has sworn that He will do so and He cannot go back on His word. He does the same for all of us. "He does not

retain his anger for ever, because he delights in steadfast love."
May His holy name be praised!

Conclusion

Conclusion

It is clear from our study of Micah that the Israelites in the eighth century BC were guilty of all the sins we are familiar with from our reading of Isaiah and the other prophets. See for example Isaiah chapter 1. Foremost was social injustice of the most venal and detestable kind. Israel's rulers detested justice (3:9). "Its heads give judgement for a bribe; its priests teach for a price; its prophets practise divination for money" (Micah 3:11). "They all lie in wait for blood, and each hunts the other with a net" (7:2). Yet they dared to say "Is not the LORD in the midst of us? No disaster shall come upon us" (3:11). Most hateful to the Lord was the scant measure, the wicked scales, and the deceitful weights, with the accompanying violence and lies (6:10-12).

Next to injustice was idolatry and the corruption of their God-given religion. Sorcery was rife and the worship of carved images (5:12-14). "Will the Lord be pleased with thousands of rams, with ten thousand rivers of oil? Shall I give my firstborn for my transgressions, the fruit of my body for the sin of my soul? He has told you, O man, what is good, and what does the Lord require of you but to do justice, and to love kindness, and to walk humbly with your God?" (6:7-8). Sacrificing their own children was the most horrific practice they had picked up from the heathen. How could the possibly imagine that their God would be appeased by such an abomination?

God's patience must have been exhausted by 700 BC if not long before, but so far as Judah was concerned it was another hundred years before He began to carry out His threats in earnest. How therefore did Micah view the future of his people? In the first chapter he predicted the destruction of Samaria along with an invasion of Judah which would reach to the gate of Jerusalem. This prophecy was fulfilled, we believe, in the sixth and fourteenth years of Hezekiah. In his sixth year Samaria was captured by Sargon, king of Assyria, and in his fourteenth year Judah was invaded by Sennacherib, Sargon's son and successor.

Micah however went on to predict the total destruction of Jerusalem and the exile of Judah's inhabitants to Babylon (3:12; 4:10). This might have been fulfilled in Micah's day, but thanks to Hezekiah's repentance and entreaties the disaster was averted at that time (Jer. 26:16-19). A hundred years later Jeremiah uttered the same warning using very much the same language as Micah himself. The people were unwilling to believe that anything of that nature would happen to them. They thought the fulfilment would be delayed as on previous occasions. They were saying, "The vision that he sees is for many days from now, and he prophesies of times far off." But Ezekiel, to whom they referred, disillusioned them. "Thus says the Lord, 'None of my words will be delayed any longer, but the word that I speak will be performed, declares the Lord God'" (Ezekiel 12:26-28).

And so it came to pass. Jerusalem was besieged in 589 BC and destroyed in 586, and the people were taken captive to Babylon as Micah had predicted.

So far so good. Allowing for postponements by God's mercy, Micah's predictions to this point were fulfilled. But he goes on to predict the birth of Christ at Bethlehem Ephrathah (5:2), the return of the exiles to the people of Israel (5:3), and their deliverance from "the Assyrian" by the One born at Bethlehem, "when he comes into our land and treads within our border" (5:5-6). All this could have happened during and immediately after the Babylonian exile, as Micah and Isaiah seem to imply. In fact, however, the birth of Christ was postponed for more than five centuries.

In the first century AD the stage was set for the fulfilment of the rest of Micah's predictions. But because the Jews rejected their Messiah and went on doing so throughout the book of Acts, there were yet more delays. The fulfilment of prophecy in general was put on hold, the Jews were dismissed until further notice, and a new dispensation was introduced in which Jew and Gentile believers become the body of Christ regardless of national (and all other) distinctions. This dispensation, after nearly two thousand years, is now drawing to a close. Before long (how long we cannot say) prophecy, the sleeping giant, will start up again, and the great mass of unfulfilled prophecy, Micah's included, will begin to be fulfilled. So far as Micah is concerned, this will include:

(1) The Lord will rescue Israel and redeem them from their enemies (4:10).
(2) The exiles will return to join those already in the land (4:10; 5:3).
(3) The Assyrian with many nations in tow will invade Israel's borders (4:11-12; 5:5).
(4) They will be annihilated by the daughter of Zion in the power of the Lord (4:12-13; 5:5-6).
(5) The Temple will be restored on an elevated site (4:1).
(6) The nations will be forcefully subdued and brought to heel (5:7-9).
(7) They will flow to Jerusalem to be taught by the Lord (4:2-3).
(8) The Lord will be their judge and arbitrator (4:3).
(9) War will not even be taught any more (4:3).
(10) The land itself will be cleansed of all that offends (5:10-14).
(11) The Lord will rule over them from Mount Zion (4:6-8; 5:4).

(12) His fame and influence will reach to the ends of the earth (5:4).

More on the Minor Prophets

Hosea: Prophet to Israel
By Charles Ozanne

Malachi: The Lord's Messenger
By Charles Ozanne

Nahum's Vision Concerning Nineveh
By Charles Ozanne

Joel and The Day of the Lord – Joel
By Charles Ozanne

Joel's Prophecy: Past and Future
By Michael Penny

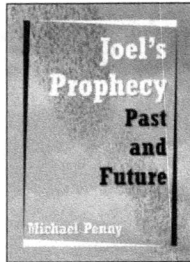

"This is a verse by verse exposition of the book of Joel, followed by a study of its application in Acts chapter 2. In his usual racy style, the author rejects the interpretation commonly held by Pentecostals and charismatics, arguing that a correct understanding can only be gained by carefully considering the original text. Helpful maps, diagrams and indexes make this book excellent value for money."
(Reviewed in *The Methodist Recorder,* UK)

Works on the Major Prophets

Isaiah 53: Who is the Suffering Servant?
Frederick Aston

Jeremiah 18:7-10: A Key to Unfulfilled Prophecy
Michael Penny

The Book of Immanuel (Isaiah 7-12)
Charles Ozanne

The Dream (Daniel 2)
Michael Penny

Daniel's Seventy Sevens
A recalculation
Michael Penny

Empires of the End-Time
Charles Ozanne

In this book the Empires of the End-Times are viewed through Daniel's telescopic lens. The uncharted end-times and the between-times of history are laid bare in Daniel's penetrating beam.

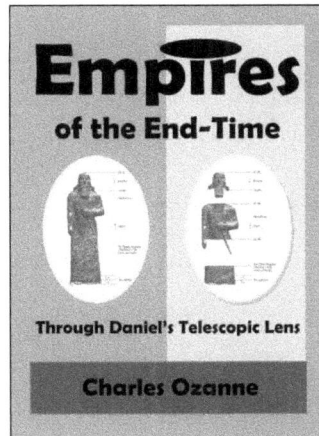

Empires of the End-Time

Through Daniel's Telescopic Lens

Charles Ozanne

More details of these books can be seen on www.obt.org.uk
and they can be ordered from www.obt.org.uk and from:

The Open Bible Trust,
Fordland Mount, Upper Basildon,
Reading, RG8 8LU, UK.

They are also available as eBooks from
Amazon Kindle and Apple

And as KDP paperbacks from Amazon.

About the author

Charles Ozanne was born in Crowborough, Sussex, in 1936. He read Theology at Oxford before undertaking research in the book of Revelation for his PhD at the University of Manchester under F. F. Bruce. Some of his recent publications for the Open Bible Trust have been a commentary on Daniel, entitled *Empires of the End-Time;* a critique of Replacement Theology entitled *God's Plan for Israel: Replacement or Restoration?* and a work looking at *The Sabbath and Circumcision.*

One of his latest works is *Understanding the New Testament,* (see next page), which is also available as an eBook. This is a well-written and well-presented commentary on the whole of the New Testament, showing that each of the 27 documents, although distinctive, fit into an overall pattern. For further details of this latest book, and his many others, please visit ...

www.obt.org.uk

Understanding

The New Testament

By Charles Ozanne

This book is written from the point of view that the New Testament is a single book made up of twenty-seven inter-related parts. Therefore, understanding something of the whole will increase our appreciation of the individual writings.

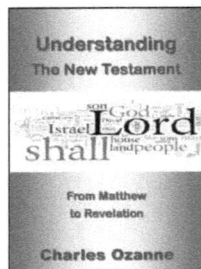

The author's desire is to give the reader *understanding*, i.e. an understanding of what the whole of the New Testament is about. With that aim in view, he gives us a guided tour through the New Testament, briefly explaining the purpose of each book in turn before giving a synopsis of its teaching.

In this way by examining the parts, the meaning of the whole becomes clearer and ... the meaning of the parts is brought more sharply into focus by understanding the whole.

More details of this book can be seen on www.obt.org.uk and they can be ordered from www.obt.org.uk and from:

The Open Bible Trust,
Fordland Mount, Upper Basildon,
Reading, RG8 8LU, UK.

It is also available as eBooks from Amazon Kindle and Apple, and as a KDP paperback from Amazon

About this book

"Who is like the Lord?"
The Meaning of Micah

After Solomon's reign, the nation of Israel was divided between ten Northern tribes and two Southern tribes. They were identified as "the house of Israel and the house of Judah". During this period the LORD raised up various prophets to speak to these two kingdoms. This was the situation when the LORD called Micah to prophesy.

Micah prophesied to the house of Israel at the same time as Isaiah was prophesying to the house of Judah. These two prophets confirm and complement one another. They major on the same themes and they are both preoccupied with the person of Christ. There was no shortage of preachers at that time, exposing the wickedness of the people and the terrible consequences of their rebellion. But their explicit warnings of coming retribution fell, by and large, on deaf ears.

Publications of The Open Bible Trust must be in accordance with its evangelical, fundamental and dispensational basis. However, beyond this minimum, writers are free to express whatever beliefs they may have as their own understanding, provided that the aim in so doing is to further the object of The Open Bible Trust. A copy of the doctrinal basis is available on **www.obt.org.uk** or from:

THE OPEN BIBLE TRUST
Fordland Mount, Upper Basildon,
Reading, RG8 8LU, UK.

www.ingramcontent.com/pod-product-compliance
Lightning Source LLC
Chambersburg PA
CBHW060722030426
42337CB00017B/2969